Scrambled Lives on Buttered Toast

Scrambled Lives on Buttered Toast

by

Ceinwen E Cariad Haydon

First published 2024 by The Hedgehog Poetry Press,

5 Coppack House, Churchill Avenue, Clevedon. BS21 6QW

www.hedgehogpress.co.uk

ISBN: 978-1-916830-14-1

Contents

I DREAMT BEING ELEANOR R AS A NUDIST

I didn't think I'd survive without clothes to hide
behind; I must have been drunk to find the courage
to join a nudist colony. To see it's great to be free.

I'd never heard of naturists before. I'm wondering,
have you? My husband's horror nearly killed him:
apoplectic and enraged – his blood pressure rose
through the roof. Once, I fancied him, but now
he isn't at all engaging, in truth. Uncertain,
insecure he doesn't like his prime possession
being on display to other men and women.
He has his status to consider; a bold leader
of nations in a modern world. He screamed,

*Eleanor, get dressed; do you not see how unseemly
your nakedness is, to me. Your belly lies in folds,
your thighs wobble, your cunt scents every chair
you sit upon. Disgusting exhibition. Crazy wife.*

I watch his irregular ugliness tumbling out
and turn away: glance at a full-length mirror –

evening's soft light licks my bevvy of curves
and I stand upright. Proud to be bare, be free of
corsets, my pendulous breasts bounce in harmony.

ENOUGH, ALREADY

For God's sake. My shoe laces are undone again,
I've lost the knack of tying tight knots.
My cup slips from my saucer, splashes
tea over my lap. My fork jabs my receded gums,
I taste blood, metallic whiffs stain my breath.
I swallow poorly-chewed toast, wishing
I might magic my teeth back to a full set.
I almost choke on a rogue crumb going down
the wrong way. My bladder squeals, *full,*
with very little warning. I dash, trip over
the rucked rug, warm wee soaks my knickers.
I hide from my neighbours, ashamed.
They press my bell, their worried faces
peer through my netted windows. I escape,
take a shower, my feet slip on soap,
I slide down, hit my head. Pass out. Blue lights
and sirens split my silent space. Urgent voices
call, before my door's kicked open. A soft-spoken
paramedic rouses me, checks I'm breathing: I'm okay
to struggle through another day of obstacles. I cry,
For God's sake, let me finish my home straight.

SLAIN

She knows the circular path well,
and walks it frequently. Six miles
of easy terrain, she barely
engages her brain to orientate.
This time, she strides out,
warmed by winter sunshine
to outpace her normal speed;
takes pleasure in her raised heart rate.

Five miles along, and ready for a mug
of steaming tea, an inert form blocks
her way. In slow motion, it makes shape:

a lifeless fawn, legs frozen akimbo,
lying on its side. One dark, doe eye
fixes her with its wide-open stare.
Soft, white fluff cuffs the creature's
death-lair, shit is strewn around its carcass.

On its side, a gaping, crimson hole –
a lethal wound,
football-sized –
spills blood, flesh,
muscles and trailing ligaments
staining surrounding clumps of grass.

She gasps, retches, rushes past
the stark, dizzying sight. Yards further on
she wonders what else she could have done
to honour the fallen deer
and its corrupted beauty. The winter sun
turns cold. Her spirit is imprinted
and she knows her dreams will unfold
perpetual images of this cruel slaughter.

FACING THE IMPLICATIONS

I found two folded five-pound notes
lying in the grass, by my path. I bent
and picked them up and looked around
to see who might have dropped them:
no-one was in sight. I fingered them
inside my coat pocket and smiled
at my good fortune. Today,

two weeks on, I've fancied
lots of stories, imagined where
that ten pounds came from

and what its loss might mean.

A child saving for their mother's
birthday; the first since her divorce.
A wealthy golfer, too lazy to turn
back to find his mislaid money.
A tired mother eking out cash
for food, until her benefits are due.
Two teenaged girls, pursuing
strawberry-flavoured vapes.
A pensioner set on a pack of fags,
his first Marlboros in a week.
Illicit gains made by a lad who taxed
a younger boy, and took his phone.
A treat kitty, held by a dad, excited
to have parental access, at last.
A papergirl's earnings for rising at six
every school day, ready for sleep.

Today, the fivers weigh heavy. Now
I want rid. I pass my corner shop,
go in, and buy two Scratch Cards.
Take my chance.

Of course,
like all the other losers -
in the end, I didn't win a thing.

SMOTHERED LOVE

Our twined lives are too big for this tiny house –
detritus gathers in corners then spills out, creeps
over floors and sofas, where dust accumulates.
My piles of books, pens and works in progress
(yours too), smudge the clean lines we planned
when we first furnished our small rooms. Worn
down, I tolerate my own mess better than yours:
see, my surfaces aren't sticky with yucky smears,
streaked by banana skins, spills, melted chocolate
droppings and crumbs. Yearly, more stuff mounts,
offering less air, less space, as taut tensions crackle
towards storms about to break. Everywhere we turn,
fumes of chaos choke us back. Our gaunt faces frown,
and mirror our manky milieu, cluttered beyond use.
One day, one of us will break out, leave our mess
and mayhem, drawn to openings, order and fresh air:

a place to create and cry; to recall our smothered love.

A PATH LESS TRAVELLED

At the crossroads, someone must have turned the signpost round:
she believed she'd followed a direct path, albeit over stony ground,
to reach her destination (the place she understood she was meant
to go). After mile upon mile, she realised she'd headed uphill
and away from promised comforts. She was truly lost, adrift.
Her tarmacked path became a muddy track, became a sheep run,
then ran out. She thought of her lover waiting, sipping slowly.
Her blood heated, flowed, freed to know how close she'd come
to bowing to imprisonment between slippy, silk sheets designed
to softly smother her sweet pride. Her stride picked up, her feet
sprang like the hooves of a mountain nanny goat. As dense fog
descended she found a cave to shelter, warmed under woodland.
She slept; dreams swirled. Finally, she owned her own strength,
saw her hand as it had moved to twirl the crucial waymark round.

SITTING ROOM

Week-old lilies, flaccid stars, cloy the air
and languish in green tinged water. A birthday gift
held for too long in a rusted metal jug.

Stones from beaches, in scattered lines contour
her wooden mantelpiece – nestled by postcards,
sea-glass, shells and shed feathers.

Stacked logs, pine-resined, await their turn
to burn. At night flames warm toes, then fade;
embers cooling to choke the grate with ashes:

Books pile high on shelves, under chairs,
in corners –
some read with care, others ignored.
One volume sits on a dusty table,
to raise a screen for Zoom.

By a sunken settee, a surface bows
beneath weights of hand cream,
lip balm, sanitiser, glasses
(too weak for milk-filmed eyes).
Also, jars of pens and tins
of unremembered things.

Cables electric gadgets
trail over rugs and floorboards.
Chargers never used in time:
devices very nearly dead.

Cupboard doors closed
on teetering stacks:
crockery, DVDs
last year's Christmas cards,

and a tatty address book, now
with many names crossed out:
desisted or deceased.

Walls are hung with pictures:
oils, acrylic, charcoal. The best,
a sketch drawn by a boy, aged seven.

An airer spread with still-damp clothes
grows fusty and stinks of yesterday's
fried potatoes. Red, cherry lights,
strung up years ago, are on the blink.

Scented candles, on the hearth,
flicker forgiving light as day drifts
onward towards night. Later,
this room will grey to morning.

AN OLD FRIEND'S PASSING

The day before she died she smiled,
her face shone with remembered youth.
Her purpled, thin-skinned hand stroked
my gardener's fingers, bestowed blessings.

Her face shone with remembered youth,
as evening softened her with falling light.
My gardener's fingers bestowed blessings
as I damped her dry lips with the water of life.

As evening softened her with falling light,
a chapel bell chimed the fleeting hours.
As I damped her dry lips with the water of life
I remembered to name death's sacrament.

A chapel bell chimed the fleeting hours.
I stroked her purpled, thin-skinned hand
and remembered to name death's sacrament.
The day before she died she smiled.

FATEFUL DAYS

1

Driving rain and gales bend her head,
sodden, she shivers and hallucinates –
home fires and loving arms, fresh food
and berried wine. Hypothermia causes
fear to slip away and her cold skin
stops aching. Cradled in a ditch
lined with wet beech leaves,

rich copper colours provoke a furnace;
she surrenders and flies towards
stars of bright light, to accept
her ancestors' welcome.

~ ~

2

A bearded face looms, his hands
shake her awake;
you're safe now –
she hears his broken words
in her second tongue. Peace flees, courage
teeters on the brink then settles down
and roots in her undernourished mind.

She determines to survive, to live
and claim her days for the children
she might bear, if war should go away.

~ ~

3

She stares this strange, new land square in the eye,
thinks how hard it will be to make it her home.
When people mis-pronounce her name, at first
she feels alone and stranded. When she's sad
she remembers how kindness saved her life,
won her time to live on. Looking outwards,
she becomes braver, speaks to others –
uses her hands and pulls expressive faces
– when the right words escape her.
Soon, she makes good friends
and one night

meets the father of her children;
a chance encounter in her local pub.
They both like red wine,
with a blackcurrant nose
and long aftertastes of coffee.

On their wedding day, to celebrate,
they quaff a new drink.
Together, they relish *champagne*.

~ ~

4

Many full years have passed. Today,
she's a widow, yet summer's sunshine relieves
her stiff joints. In her handkerchief-sized garden
her grandchildren make mud pies
and sing the old songs of her motherland.
She has taught them well
to know their heritage.
She recalls how once, overwhelmed
by hell, she was tempted to die too early.

Next time she sees the vivid light of afterlife,
she'll fly towards it, sanctified by blessings
bubbled by streams of laughter.
At length, intoxicated by her life,
she'll float away, like on that precious day
when she sipped her first *coupe de champagne brut.*

~ ~

DISTURBED

You fill my willingness with shrill
outpourings, dwindle brilliance
into fragile fly-by-nights. You
trill daylight into luminescence,
lullaby me every lunar night.
Loquacious lunatics listen,
spellbound, to stellar symphonies.
Will my fullness illuminate new lands,
leverage my legacy as I till loamy
virgin soil? Can I lessen
my ego and lay zeal to rest –